MY PUBLISHING
IMPRINT

Also in the *Countdown to Book Launch*™ Series

- Reference essential metadata details for ISBNs, barcodes, LCCNs, copyright.
- Avoid legal headaches, missed deadlines, and expensive fees.
- Learn how to publish as a professional, not an amateur.
- Protect your book's hard-earned reader reviews.
- Ensure your freedom to use any book printer.
- Include your book in the directories used by major publishers.
- Keep your options open to use any book distributor.
- Prevent your advance reading copies from being re-sold online.

Learn more at www.DavidWogahn.com/ryb

Book Reviews: Step One on the Road to Book Sales

Learn more at www.DavidWogahn.com/brc

Also by David Wogahn

The Book Reviewer Yellow Pages, 9th Edition
Successful eBook Publishing
Marketing and Distributing eBooks
(LinkedIn Learning)

MY PUBLISHING IMPRINT

How to Create a Self-Publishing Book Imprint & ISBN Essentials

Countdown to Book Launch™, Book 1

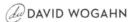 DAVID WOGAHN

PartnerPress
Carlsbad, California

My Publishing Imprint:
How to Create a Self-Publishing Book Imprint & ISBN Essentials
© 2020 David Wogahn, All Rights Reserved.

www.DavidWogahn.com

Available in these formats:
- 978-1-944098-12-4 (Paperback)
- 978-1-944098-13-1 (eBook)
- 978-1-944098-16-2 (Audiobook)

Library of Congress Control Number: 2019945451

Editing: Katie Barry
Cover design: Anton Stefanov Rangelov
Publishing Services: Kerri Esten, AuthorImprints
Audiobook producer: Carter Wogahn

Published by PartnerPress | Carlsbad, California

For volume and resale pricing, please contact publish@partnerpress.org

Rivers are easiest to cross at their source.

— Publilius Syrus,
The Moral Sayings of Publius Syrus:
A Roman Slave

Contents

The Countdown to Book Launch™ Series

The Countdown to Book Launch series is for authors, self-publishers, and small presses with limited time and a need for authoritative publishing information informed by real-world experience. Each book focuses on its intended topic and avoids fluff or filler material.

For the past ten years, my company, AuthorImprints, has managed the publication of more than 200 books on behalf of self-publishers. It is that experience and learning that I present here for the benefit of fiction and nonfiction authors alike.

But as it can be with how-to guides, information and resource links are subject to change. I help readers cope with this in two unique ways.

1. Hyperlinks to online references in each book are replaced with a URL link shortener domain: breve.link. It works like Bitly or TinyURL; long,

complicated links are replaced with easy-to-read and maintain links. It allows us to keep the links in your book working and makes it easier to look-up links if you are reading the paperback. More on this in the first chapter.

2. Members of my mailing list receive advance notice about exclusive launch offers when I release a book or training resource. Join my mailing list at:

DavidWogahn.com/join

or subscribe to one of the free resources at AuthorImprints.com to be notified.

To your success,
David Wogahn

DavidWogahn.com
AuthorImprints.com

Important Notice about CreateSpace

I n August 2018 Amazon announced the closure of CreateSpace print-on-demand (POD) and began moving all accounts to a new paperback POD service available from Kindle Direct Publishing (KDP) called KDP Print. The services are nearly identical as they relate to the topics of this book with the notable exception of the name of your publisher, should you choose the free ISBN option.

If you choose the free ISBN from KDP Print, the *published by* name for your book will now read "Independently published" instead of "CreateSpace Independent Publishing Platform." All book industry databases will show this publisher name, not just your book listing on Amazon.

CreateSpace was so entrenched that you are likely to come across references to it for years to come. That also means tens of thousands of books will continue to use the CreateSpace ISBN and the published by name of CreateSpace Independent Publishing Platform...forever.

When you do come across references to CreateSpace outside of Amazon, you can assume what they are saying also applies to KDP Print. Either they haven't updated their information, or they don't know about the change.

Part 1

Introduction: Publishing Imprints

Indie publishing has gone pro. It is no longer the poor stepchild of publishing, the last resort for an author who isn't "chosen" by a traditional publisher. But what does this mean?

We all know the importance of book covers, editing, and the writing itself. But lately I've seen emphasis placed on the business aspects of indie publishing, from the type of entity we choose (LLC, corporation, sole proprietor), to how we track our expenses and budget our marketing investments.

Wayne Stinnett, a self-described trucker turned best-selling novelist in two years, shares this sage advice from his nonfiction book, *Blue Collar to No Collar*:

> *Make no mistake, if you're an indie, you are more than just a writer. You're the publisher. You only*

publish one author, but that doesn't change the fact that you are a businessperson.

Since 2012, the year I began working exclusively with small publishers, I've helped more than 100 authors create their own publishing imprints (this guide, and many in the industry, use self- and indie publishing interchangeably). Some of these were formed as corporations and LLCs, but most were in name only. The common thread between all of them—one of the earliest decisions made—was to choose a name under which to buy an ISBN, short for International Standard Book Number, a unique number assigned to published books.

Early in the eBook revolution Amazon declared eBooks did not need an ISBN. Much to the consternation of Bowker (the official U.S.-issuer of ISBNs), and the publishing industry itself, eBook self-publishing platforms had no choice but to follow Amazon's lead. Even Apple, which launched iBooks by requiring an ISBN for eBooks, was forced to abandon its position.

"Who cares?" many new publishers declared as they forged ahead. Bowker did not/does not adequately explain the value of assigning one, so what's the point? I can't argue with them.

But like the other technology-fueled revolutions of the past 30 years, publishing is becoming more sophisticated. Print-on-demand—which does require an ISBN—is used by publishers large and small. Wholesale distribution for author-published books is thriving. Online eBook promotion companies have attracted venture capital.

And what's driving the embrace of these new services and vendors? Break-out author-publishers striking out to create their own "mini" publishing empires.

- Barbara Freethy's **Hyde Street Press**
- Huge Howie's **Broad Reach Publishing**
- Meredith Wild's **Waterhouse Press**

Even businesses such as The McKinsey Global Institute, the Content Marketing Institute, and Ars Technica have their own book publishing imprints.

Why this book

Being present at the beginning of the PC revolution in 1983 and the internet in 1992, I witnessed firsthand how quickly traditional industry hierarchies were flattened. Entire middle layers of companies, technologies and services simply evaporated. However, what always remained were a few industry standards or practices that helped pave the way for new entrants, so they could compete with entrenched incumbents.

In our little corner of the publishing world, the ISBN is one of those quaint relics that even Amazon can't extinguish or co-op. I began thinking about what value it provides the author/publisher, and what the consequences are for using, or not using, one.

Most importantly, I wondered how our decisions in this area reflected on our publishing brands. What did it mean for lasting value? Who sees this information? How is it interpreted by the media and public?

What does it mean to those who have discovered they can have the business of their dreams rather than moonlighting; living in the shadows of "big publishing?"

I know this may seem like minutia to new writers. But I've learned that these early decisions can and do have a long-term impact with little or no chance for fixing or correcting, short of re-publishing.

Is a lack of planning or investment fatal? Of course not. But it is much easier if you understand those implications early so you can make an informed decision.

That's what this book is about. I wrote *My Publishing Imprint* to help authors understand their options and the consequences of their decisions. There is a lot of misinformation floating around and I hope this little book becomes a guidepost for those looking to set off on the right foot.

So, let's do that. Let's see what "going pro" looks like for indie publishers. If it makes sense for your situation, you'll learn here what you need to do to ensure you've built a firm foundation upon which to build your publishing venture.

1

What Is a Publishing Imprint?

A publishing imprint is the name of your publishing company. This name is:

- Displayed to the public wherever you sell your book.
- Recorded in book industry databases used by retailers, book wholesalers, and book distributors.
- Listed on your book's copyright page, and often included in your book's sales and promotional materials.
- The name assigned to your ISBN(s).

It can be an invented name or the name of one's existing business, or some variation. New publishers can use their author name, but I think it is preferable to create a distinction between the author name and the publisher for public relations and brand-building reasons.

In the last ten years, books that use an ISBN registered by small publishing imprints (Bowker calls them Small Publishers) increased 205%—from 14,952 in 2008 to 45,649 in 2017.

The first question that usually follows is: Do I need to set up a company under this name? The short answer is that there is no requirement, but depending on your circumstances, it might make sense.

One consideration is whether you want to accept payment in the name of your imprint. Financial institutions will want to see proof that you are authorized to be "doing business as" (DBA) this name, so you will need to formally register the *fictitious* name. Check with your city, county, or state, and consult your tax or legal adviser about your individual circumstances.

Why make this decision early

You can certainly skip this step, do it just before your book's release date, or after you've already published a few books. But I believe you want to decide on a name for your imprint early for one important reason:

Marketing a book before its release date—sending out advance reader copies (ARCs) to get reviews and blurbs—is one of the most effective marketing activities you can do. You will be promoting your ARCs and doing pre-publication PR using the name of your imprint.

Another reason to consider selecting your name early is that it is an important metadata element. Depending on the words it may help your book show up in search results—on Google as well as Amazon.

Why choose a name other than your own?

As noted above, a name other than your own helps create (and maintain) a public record separate from you the author. As many of us know there continues to be a bias by many in the media, book retailers, and some readers against self-published books. A unique name, with no ties to your own, could help your marketing efforts. It certainly won't hinder your marketing like the use of your own name as an imprint name might.

Is this considered unethical or deceitful? No! You are no different than any other small business seeking a future of self-determination. Many writers dream about writing full-time. And I think it helps authors maintain a healthy distinction between us as writers and us as business owners. It may also be helpful in establishing the legitimacy of your business when it comes to filing taxes.

Are you a hobbyist or a business?

Where is your publishing imprint name used?

Here are five key places an imprint name can appear or be used, many of them publicly visible:

1. **Books In Print,** the official registry of U.S.-published books. Maintained by Bowker, this is the sole company authorized to sell ISBNs in the U.S.
2. **Library of Congress** filing. Besides the imprint name, you need your publisher identifier from your ISBN series to start the process. The publisher name you enter must be the same as the one you entered as publisher when you bought the ISBN. (The free ISBNs issued by CreateSpace, KDP Print, and IngramSpark do not qualify.)
3. **Distribution accounts** through services such as IngramSpark and KDP Print. This is especially relevant if you plan to enable pre-release ordering for your book, which means you need to choose a name before beginning the process.
4. **Book sales pages** setup by individual retailers, such as Amazon. This displays automatically

for books available via pre-order (e.g., Amazon Advantage or IngramSpark).

5. **Business filings:** Banking and other account setups.

Many best-selling authors ignore this topic

It would be disingenuous for me to say that you must have a publishing imprint or that the name associated with the ISBN is important for sales success. For the record, here are several successful authors that find little need for imprint names and ISBN ownership:

- Bella Forrest
- Chris Fox
- K.F. Breene
- Mark Dawson
- Patrick King
- Quinn Loftis

These author-publishers use the free ISBN provided by CreateSpace and KDP Print so their paperbacks show a publishing imprint name of "CreateSpace Independent Publishing Platform" or, in the case of KDP Print, "Independently published." Both are publishing imprint names that Amazon chose when they purchased ISBNs from Bowker for purposes of providing them free to author-publishers.

That's the operative word: *free*. This choice does not seem to have reduced or hindered the success of these authors. In fact, the free Amazon ISBN was assigned to 751,924 paperbacks in 2017.

Which is the right path for you and your book? This is what you need to decide. Again, it is a decision you make once, and it cannot be changed without re-publishing your book. Now let's continue.

Do you need a website for your imprint?

Most likely, no. You certainly don't need one in the beginning when budgets are tight, and every dollar should go to building your author platform and creating the highest quality book possible. Ultimately, an imprint website depends on your goals and resources.

You can start out by just buying the domain name. Beyond owning one, the next step in expense and complexity is connecting it to an email address. For example, publisher@[yournamehere].com. Or you can level-up to a website once you feel you have the books—or stable of authors—to support a dedicated website.

If or when you do decide to invest, this website can remain simple. For example, the minimum requirements are:

- Book covers and brief metadata for all the books published under your imprint.
- A reference to where the books can be purchased.
- A media kit for each book (press release, author Q&A, reviews, blurbs, author bio, an excerpt or chapter).
- A link to your main website and book websites, if any.
- A reference for contacting the publisher for review copies.
- A reference for contacting the publisher to reach the author about speaking, writing, or interview opportunities.

In other words, this becomes a funnel for PR activity. If you have a publicist, great. If not, this can serve as a presence to receive public relations inquiries 24-7.

A twist on this idea is something I provide for a few AuthorImprints clients. PartnerPress.org is our publishing imprint and it has several pages for books by authors with their own imprints. When someone types that imprint name into their browser, they are redirected to a page on PartnerPress.org. Check out http://www.goodpressbooks.com to see how it works.

2

Legal Matters and Considerations

Years ago, my business school professor asked us a question: "Who here wants to have their own business?" Most of us raised our hands. "Okay," he said, "You're in business."

His point was that "being in business" was simple. All we had to do was say that we were in business.

Of course, we all know that the next step is to answer several important questions such as: What if we want legal protection? What happens at tax time? What name do we use to open bank accounts? What about accepting payments?

What follows are some of the key considerations and answers to the questions I hear most frequently about this topic. Disclaimer: I am not an attorney or tax advisor, and rules in this area vary by location and change over time. Also, the examples and references below are United States-specific. Seek out a qualified professional where you live, someone familiar with local laws and your individual circumstances. Trust me, you'll sleep better.

Names and entities

Matters are greatly simplified when we use our own name to conduct business. Chances are everyone reading this book has a bank account in their name. You got that by proving your identity and providing a tax identification number such as your Social Security Number if you live in the U.S.

When someone writes you a check to buy your book, they can make the check out in your name. It works the same way when setting up a PayPal account or your accounts with Amazon to sell books.

Choosing a publishing imprint name works a little differently. There are no automated checks or verifications made by the three main entities where you'll enter your imprint name.

- Bowker (MyIdentifiers.com), where you register and buy your ISBNs, will ask for the imprint name. There is no cross-checking to verify your right to use that name.

- Amazon's Kindle Direct Publishing (KDP) and IngramSpark have a field for publisher name, and you enter your choice here. Again, there is no cross-checking to verify your right to use that name.

Where it does get tricky is if you want to use a name other than your own to accept payment. This is true whether you are completing the banking information profile on Amazon or selling your book at the local street fair.

Doing business as (DBA)

As I already pointed out, you don't have to go through the effort of establishing a legal entity to publish a book. Buy your ISBN(s) in the name of your imprint and use your personal bank account to accept money (checks or direct deposit).

But if you think you might want or need to do business under a name other than your own, your life will be much simpler if you make that leap now. Once your ISBNs are bought, and the book is published, the name cannot be changed. Using a new name will also require you to change all your accounts.

Here are the steps necessary to do business under a fictitious name in California. Your location may require different steps, but it is likely similar in scope. (Be sure to check for the specifics in your particular location.)

1. Research a name to make sure no one is using it.
2. File the paperwork to use your preferred fictitious name. (In California this is done at the county level; check your local laws.)
3. Publish it in an approved publication and wait a prescribed waiting period. (Easy. My county records office gives us the names of approved publications. The cost to publish the notice of intent to use a fictitious name cost me about $20.)
4. Once approved (i.e., no one protested), take the paperwork to a bank to open an account.
5. Buy ISBN(s) using this name.
6. Open online accounts with Amazon, etc., using this new name.

Contrast this with simply using your name. In that case, you skip Steps 1 to 5 because you already have an account in your name. Buy ISBNs using your imprint name. Done.

However, before filing for a DBA there is one more consideration: Do you want to do business as a sole proprietor or a legal entity?

S corp, C corp, LLC, sole proprietor?

Each of these has pros and cons and only you and your tax or legal advisor can make this decision. Together you'll likely consider liability exposure, how you plan to fund or invest in your imprint, tax consequences, royalty and expense tracking, and other factors.

What should you do? All I can tell you is that the type of entity doesn't matter to Bowker—the organization (in the U.S.) that is selling you your ISBN. It also doesn't matter to Amazon or other online stores assuming you are able to complete their banking and tax ID information.

As I said earlier, the name you use for your publishing imprint does not have to match the name you enter when completing your banking and tax information.

Tax ID numbers

If you create a legal entity like an S corporation, C corporation, or LLC you will receive a federal employer identification number (EIN)—even if you are the sole owner. You'll use this for filing taxes, opening a bank account, and will provide it when requested by companies like Amazon.

But if you decide to operate under your name or as a sole proprietor under a fictitious name, you still might consider getting an EIN rather than use your Social Security Number. It is imperative you maintain business records and reporting separate from your personal accounts, and an EIN can help do that. It also keeps your Social Security Number more secure by reducing its use in public records.

An EIN is free to obtain. Simply do a search for *employer identification number* or visit http://breve.link/mpi1.

Banking and accepting payments

If you decided to form a legal entity and/or do business under a fictitious name, you'll need a separate bank account into which you can make deposits. Early in the process you'll want to visit a bank and ask for a list of items you'll be required to provide for an account setup.

It works the same way with PayPal and other online payment vendors. Research what is required and get those in order before you begin applying for an account.

Just make sure you allow plenty of time since these steps can take days if not weeks to complete.

3

How to Choose a Name

While I can't help you come up with a specific name, I can point you to several resources to check before you get your heart set on using it for your publishing imprint. Remember that you can also add common publishing-related words like Press and Publishing to a chosen word or phrase to help distinguish it from similar names. (But don't add Inc, Corp, or LLC unless you are a legally registered entity that can use such terms.)

A few rules or guidelines about choosing names

1. Do not use trademarked terms.
2. The more unique, the better.
3. Modify a term to make it yours but avoid anything similar to a trademarked term. When in doubt, consult a lawyer. For example, one of our

clients was using *Beliefs of the Heart* so we simply added the word *Press* after the name and bought ISBNs with the imprint name of *Beliefs of the Heart Press*.

Personally, I also try to avoid special characters such as a hyphen and apostrophe. Here's a good test: Imagine you are calling your friend to tell her the name of your new publishing imprint. How many times do you have to say it, or even spell it, before she understands?

Ten resources for researching book imprint names

What makes choosing a name difficult is that there is no single place to check to see if it is in use. Some names are used simply as imprint names, so you won't find those in legal filings. That means you need to check a variety of sources where a name might be in use.

I've arranged the list below in the order that a name might turn up if it is used as a book imprint. We'll start with the most specific, the Global Register of Publishers database, and end with the most general advice I can give: contact an attorney.

Is an attorney necessary? That depends on what you have at stake, your goals, perhaps your resources, and even your confidence in your research skills.

1. Global Register of Publishers

The Global Register of Publishers is located on the ISBN International website and allows you to search publisher names worldwide. Searches return information about the publisher and a list of ISBN identifiers.

There are three things to note about searching this database:

1. Results are from around the world. If a name is used in a foreign country, it may not impact your use of the name in your country. At the same time, it could impact your use if you wanted to sell books under your name in that foreign country.
2. Bowker allows you to add additional imprint names to your ISBN account at MyIdentifiers. com, and these imprint names do not show up in this database.
3. Based on my experience, new imprints are not immediately reflected in this database. There appears to be a lag of a few months. This only means you cannot completely rely on this

database as a definitive resource. (You have nine other options so keep looking.)

http://breve.link/mpi2

2. Amazon.com

Not many people know this, but the publisher name is searchable in Amazon's search engine, even if you have one book. This makes Amazon one of the best places to find out if someone is already using an imprint name.

Unfortunately, this can be a tedious exercise depending on how unique your name is. You may see just a couple books, or pages of books. You will have to look at each book listing, scroll down to publisher, and look at that book's information.

Product details

Imprint name: every print book has one.

Paperback: 256 pages
Publisher: PartnerPress.org; edition (November 14, 2017)
Language: English
ISBN-10: 1944098089
ISBN-13: 978-1944098087

https://www.amazon.com/

TIP: Select the Books category before typing your imprint name idea. Every print book will show an imprint name.

3. GoDaddy.com

I put GoDaddy third on the list because I feel it is important to also own the domain name for one's imprint. The domain does not have to match the name exactly, nor do you need a publishing imprint website, but it is nice to have.

Websites ending in ".com" are always the first choice, but other extensions such as .net, .org, and so forth may also work. Try a few combinations and then come back to buy it after you finalize your name. Do not wait to do this.

https://www.godaddy.com/

4. Local records

Searching local government databases is required if you plan to file a fictitious name filing, or DBA. Your location may differ but, in my county (San Diego), I can search online and then visit a local office to file the necessary forms to begin the process.

5. Your secretary of state

Each state maintains a database of fictitious names that should be searched to help you avoid choosing an already-in-use name.

Search online for your state's database. For example, here is the link for California: http://breve.link/mpi3.

6. U.S. federal trademark office

Even if you do not plan to file for trademark protection, the U.S. registered trademark database at the U.S. Patent and Trademark Office (USPTO) is a good resource. Your state's trademark database may also be worth checking.

http://breve.link/mpi4

7. Literary Market Place

The Literary Market Place maintains a collection of book publishing industry databases with listings for more than 2,000 large and small publishers. It isn't as comprehensive as the Global Register of Publishers, but it is still worth checking and might even give you ideas for alternative names. Register for free and do a name search.

http://breve.link/mpi5

8. PublishersArchive.com

Like Literary Market Place, PublishersArchive.com maintains an online directory of publishers. They don't publicize the number of publishers in their database, and it is not exhaustive, but it is another place to look for already-used-names.

I especially like how you can search for publishers by state or genre. Again, these are good ways to research ideas for names as well.

https://publishersarchive.com/

9. Google search

I imagine this is where most people begin their search, but it can also be like drinking from a firehose. The search results can be never ending, and you can't always be certain about the accuracy of the results.

 Enter your search term both with and without spaces, put quotes around the term (to find an exact match), and go beyond the first few pages of results.

10. Hire an attorney

Finally, if you have more money than time—or you want to be absolutely certain—hire someone who specializes in this kind of research. Once complete, they can file all the forms on your behalf. A qualified trademark attorney has the relevant background to conduct a thorough search and all the better if they have publishing experience.

4

Branding and Positioning Considerations

The author Patrick King dominates the category of relationship and personal development books, especially for millennials. He has several top-selling books in multiple formats—Kindle, paperback, and audiobook.

Interestingly, I was surprised to see that his paperback "publisher" is CreateSpace Independent Publishing, which means he uses their free ISBN.

Does this reflect poorly on Patrick? There are many in the indie publishing community who say that the average reader doesn't care who the publisher is. How many of us even bother to scroll down to the product details on Amazon where the name is listed?

If it doesn't matter to the reader, why should it matter to you?

Whether you invest in an imprint or not comes down to your branding and positioning objectives, and how you plan to market your books.

I'd venture to say that there is no bookstore in America that is willing to order books from Amazon for an author-reading event. Bookstores do not like Amazon and they know who owns the CreateSpace and KDP Print publishing imprints.

What if you are building a personal brand, or have a business that offers products or services related to the subject of your book? Perhaps it makes sense to brand your books in a way that relates to and enhances these other ventures. This is what Sam Williamson did when he named his publishing imprint Beliefs of the Heart Press, and what the Content Marketing Institute did when it bought ISBNs in its name.

An imprint using your personal name or books published using a free ISBN from KDP Print screams "self-published." If you are approaching media outlets for interviews, which publisher sounds more professional: Waterhouse Press or Meredith Wild?

If branding is at all important, spend the $100 or so to buy at least one ISBN (or 10 for $295). Buy it using an imprint name that has meaning to you and meets the objectives of your publishing venture.

5

Profiles of Indie Publishing Imprints

Again, creating an author imprint does not have to be a costly or complex endeavor. Pick a name, buy your ISBNs, done.

The key is to be intentional about choosing, and using, the imprint name, and to do this before buying your ISBN (more on that in Part 2). With this in place, the sky is the limit and your options unfold.

Here are profiles of four authors that began publishing like you and me. They had ideas for a book and put in place the foundation upon which they continue to build their publishing businesses. One has been the subject of a *New York Times* article, while the others are imprints few have ever heard of.

OneEarth Publishing, Lee Van Ham

Lee Van Ham is a retired minister living in Southern California with a passion for educating people about what he calls "one earth living" via the OneEarth Project.

He set out to write a three-book series in 2014 and I recommended buying a block of 10 ISBNs so we could brand his books with the imprint name OneEarth Publishing. Little did we know that this imprint would soon be home to books from two other authors.

Following the publication of his second book in the series, one of his colleagues contacted me about publishing her book. Seeing that it held similar values as Lee's two other books, I suggested to the author and Lee that they use OneEarth Publishing as the imprint rather than buy additional ISBNs.

A second client referral by Lee resulted in the same outcome. This was also a nonfiction book that shared the same values of the other three books under this imprint.

Today, there are three different authors with books published under this imprint. There are no legal entanglements, and copyright is owned by each author. Even the Amazon accounts are set up in the names of each author, not the imprint.

The authors have banded together for one market-ing event and are planning to do more. Visit Ama-zon, go to the Books section in the search bar, and do a search for *oneearth publishing* to see a list of the books.

Waterhouse Press, Meredith Wild

Meredith Wild has been widely written about as a self-publishing success story. What started out as simply an imprint name—created to help gain the respect of the media and retailers—has turned into a full-service publishing enterprise.

As of late 2017, Waterhouse was the publisher for twelve other writers, including Helen Hardt and Audrey Carlan. This has enabled the imprint to reach enough volume to secure a print book distribution arrangement with Ingram Publisher Services.[1]

Learn more about Waterhouse Press by reading this interview with Shelf Awareness: http://breve.link/mpi7

Golightly Publishing, Barbara Light Lacy

You might call Barbara a serial media-preneuer. Publishing, to her, is primarily a hobby and passion. She has published six books on her own, and four with a co-author, not to mention four music CDs featuring music she wrote and performed.

When Barbara embarked on a series of books with her co-author, she felt it would be better to publish those under the name of a different imprint. As you see below, her primary imprint is Golightly Publishing and she added Rising Times Books for her co-authored series.

Contrast this with Lee Van Ham's OneEarth Publishing where he invited similar authors to share his brand, the name of his imprint. This is simply a matter of choice, depending on your publishing strategy and objectives.

How to add another imprint

After buying your ISBNs from the MyIdentifiers website (explained in Part 2), navigate to their My Company page where you will find the Add Imprint field and button. Enter your additional imprint name and click enter.

Down Island Press, Wayne Stinnett

The focus of my final profile deals with the business rationale of establishing an imprint. In the introduction I shared a quote from the novelist Wayne Stinnett, and here he expands on his business-minded approach to indie publishing. In his words:

"One of the main driving points for me to create my own imprint—using my own ISBNs for both eBooks and paperbacks—is legacy. I'm about to turn 60 and my writing will hopefully outlive me.

"Down Island Press owns the rights to my books. How the business and its assets (including book rights) is divided after I'm gone is spelled out in my will. This will allow my family to continue to earn income from them and the transition is seamless and simple."

Do you need a publishing logo for your imprint?

I highly recommend you create one. If you've gone so far as to purchase ISBNs in the name of the imprint, it doesn't take much more effort or expense to add a little style to the name you've chosen and it adds a nice professional touch.

- Use a fancy font or other font characteristic.
- Put the name inside a box or circle.
- Put the initials inside a box or circle.
- Ask your cover designer if he or she will help.

- If you want to take it up a notch, hire a designer or buy a Fiverr gig for a few dollars.

Just don't overthink it and be consistent when using it. This is something that can be changed later.

You can use it:

- On the book's spine.
- The book's back cover.
- The book's title page and/or copyright page.
- Your book's marketing materials.

Summary of Part 1

Does this sound time-consuming and involved? Perhaps, but the imprint is a name that represents us and is the brand behind our books. Once chosen, a publishing imprint name is essentially forever.

Here is a multi-step decision guide to walk you through the process of deciding.

Step 1: Do you want to use a publishing imprint name?

- If you do, go to Step 2.
- If you don't, you are done. You will be using the free ISBNs provided by Amazon, assuming you are producing a print book. If you publish in eBook-only format, you don't need an ISBN. (However, be sure to read Part 2 which explains the pros and cons of the free ISBN.)

Step 2: Decide whether you will *do business as* the name of your imprint. In other words, do you want to have a bank account in the name of your imprint and be paid using that name?

- If yes, go to Step 3a.
- If no, go to Step 3b.

Step 3a: Research names (Chapter 3). Your research will need to be more thorough if you are opening a bank account. Also, this will take more time and cost money for business filings. When done, go to Step 4.

Step 3b: Research names (Chapter 3). After you are confident of your choice, use it to buy ISBNs. See Part 2.

Step 4: Since you are using the name for a business, what type of entity will you use: LLC, corporation, sole proprietor, partnership? Discuss your options with your tax or legal advisor. Once you decide, follow their advice for the next steps.

Step 5: After you have decided on the type of entity and formal name, use it to buy ISBNs. See Part 2.

Part 2
Introduction: The International Standard Book Number

Why, when, and how to use an ISBN is a source of confusion for many new to publishing. I'd add that new publishers can also waste money, miss out on branding opportunities, and sometimes even harm their book's listing on Amazon by not understanding how the ISBN works.

The International Standard Book Number (ISBN) is an international numbering system for books, and there is only one entity authorized to issue ISBNs in each country. Some choose to charge, like the official U.S. agency (Bowker) does; others provide ISBNs for free, as is the case with Canada's agency.

Numbers are assigned to each specific format of a book and never reused. Like golf, the rules are made-up and simple, but can be misinterpreted or applied incorrectly.

Add to this that in a market where Amazon dominates, it is mighty difficult to justify the expense. It isn't like Bowker has demonstrated the ISBN's value to small publishers.

So why do we need to at least understand this important number? Here's a quick summary before we dive into the details.

ISBNs and Amazon

An ISBN is not required by Amazon to publish a Kindle eBook. If you have one, I recommend you use it and will explain why later in this section. Print, however, is a different story.

Every printed book, whether it's sold online or in stores, needs an ISBN. KDP Print will give you one for free, and I'll explain the trade-offs for taking advantage of this.

ISBNs and Google

When you type an ISBN into Google, the book it is assigned to shows up. But how many people go around with lists of ISBNs to look up? You wouldn't give out the ISBN of your book during a speech, thinking it the easier way for people to find your book.

On the other hand, Google loves standards and has been slowly implementing features to their search engine that *might* make the ISBN more relevant to searching. In that case what we really want to know is whether there is some search engine optimization (SEO) advantage to owning and using an ISBN.

As of now, there isn't any compelling evidence of SEO value.

ISBNs and printing

A company printing your book does not care whether you do or don't have an ISBN. However, a company involved in getting your book into stores or listed in online stores does care—an ISBN is required.

- Amazon's KDP Print is a printer *and* they list your book in their stores. An ISBN is required.
- IngramSpark is a printer but they give you the option of listing your book in stores. Therefore, an ISBN is optional.

It all comes down to how you plan to sell your book.

 Determine your distribution plan before you choose your printer, not the other way around.

A branding opportunity

The name of your publishing imprint might be important to your personal brand or business. If so, use it when you buy ISBNs because once it is assigned, it cannot be changed.

ISBN records are distributed to all sorts of databases, some of which are searched by book retailers and libraries. Depending on your goals, strategy, and marketing plans, this could be important.

Worldwide standard

As I mentioned above, this number is recognized worldwide as the only way to identify books sold through stores. That means that you don't need a different ISBN to sell your book in the UK or Germany, for example.

The only time you need a different ISBN to sell in an international market is if the publisher, language, or format of the book changes. A book written in English, published by the same publisher, and using the same format may be sold anywhere in the world (assuming the publisher owns worldwide rights).

Free ISBNs

An ISBN that lists someone else as the publisher—the free KDP Print ISBN for example—has nothing to do with copyright. I think of it more as a branding opportunity for Amazon (who owns KDP Print) and a lost opportunity for the author–publisher.

An ISBN for print books may also lock you into using the printer that provided the ISBN. For example, using the free KDP Print ISBN, you agree not to print your book using any other printer except KDP Print (or CreateSpace; read your contract for details and limitations).

6

Nine ISBN Fundamentals

et's begin by defining some key terms and then I'll address frequently asked questions organized into nine topics.

ASIN, Amazon Standard Identification Number. A ten-digit proprietary number Amazon uses to identify what they sell, including non-book products. You see it used in the product description under **Product Details** for all books.

- Kindle eBooks: They never display an ISBN, even if you enter one into KDP. It is always the ASIN.
- Print books: In Amazon-speak, they use ASIN and ISBN interchangeably. It isn't something for us to be concerned about; just be aware of it.

Assignment/Assigned/Assigning. An ISBN is called *assigned* once a book is formally published.

This happens automatically if you select Amazon's free ISBN or if you buy the ISBN from a reseller like Amazon or IngramSpark.

Otherwise you must manually enter the minimum required details about a book for the ISBN it is using. This is done using your account at MyIdentifiers.com (for U.S.-based publishers).

EAN, International Article Number (also known as European Article Number). A standard that describes the numbering system used in world trade. The ISBN is part of this standard as is the Universal Product Code or UPC. Some Amazon documentation will use ISBN and EAN interchangeably (e.g., EIN-13 is the same as ISBN-13).

Format. The physical or virtual format of the book. Common examples include hardcover, paperback, eBook, spiral bound, CD-ROM, and so on.

ISBN, International Standard Book Number. I recall receiving an email from a new client saying, "I've studied the differences between the ISBN-13 and ISBN-10 and I think I'm going to go with the ISBN-13."

He didn't realize that they are the same number.

The only number you can buy is the ISBN-13. When originally introduced in the early 1960s, it was ten digits, the ISBN-10. As the available numbers dwindled, the international agency simply increased it by three numbers in a way that allowed the two to co-exist.

You can convert a ISBN-10 to a ISBN-13, and ISBN-13 to a ISBN-10 using this tool: http://breve.link/mpi8

KDP, Kindle Direct Publishing. Amazon's self-service publishing portal. It is free to use for publishing Kindle eBooks and paperback books in various Amazon marketplaces around the world.

Metadata. The details that describe a book such as title, author name, trim size, page count, price, and format.

Trim or trim size. A book's height and width dimensions, such as 6" wide by 9" tall.

1. eBooks and ISBNs

One of the first things new publishers learn is that they don't need to use an ISBN for their eBook. However, this is only part of the story, and it pays to understand the bigger picture before you cross this off your list as done.

The ISBN golden rules of books in any format, whether paperback, hardcover, or eBook, are:

1. The ISBN requirement is up to the store or entity that is selling or distributing the book.

2. A new and unique ISBN is assigned to each version of a book.

For example, Amazon's KDP does not require an ISBN because they assign their own number called an ASIN. IngramSpark requires publishers to provide their own ISBN. You can also have a distributor like Draft2Digital that requires an ISBN but will assign one of theirs if you don't have one. Herein lies the problem.

As we discussed earlier, the imprint name will show up in online databases, most of which are not stores where the book is sold. If you use a free ISBN provided by someone like Draft2Digital or Smashwords, your books will show them as the publisher. Also keep in mind that if you stop using their service, you cannot continue to use their ISBN.

Perhaps this isn't a big deal to you, but if you are trying to build a brand it is something you should be aware of. My advice about assigning an ISBN to an eBook is to use an ISBN if you bought them in the name of your imprint. This number will also be placed on your copyright page.

Alternatively, if you want to conserve your supply of numbers *and* you are distributing directly to Amazon, Barnes & Noble, Apple, and/or Kobo, you can skip it and add one later.

Two more things

You don't need to assign a separate (unique) ISBN to both the EPUB file and Mobi (Kindle) file.[2] It is true that they are separate file formats that may differ from each other—thus requiring a unique ISBN—but they won't be sold in the same store as a paperback and hardcover could be sold.

Finally, there is no such thing as an "eISBN" or special "varieties" of ISBNs. In fact, a game, toy, or stuffed animal can have an ISBN.

2. Print books and ISBNs

Back to our golden rules: (1) the need for an ISBN is up to the store or book distributor and (2) a new and unique ISBN is assigned to each version of a book.

I have a client who publishes workbooks used in her consulting practice. She sells them directly from her website or gives them away as part of her consulting service.

In her case she uses IngramSpark, rather than KDP Print, because IngramSpark gives authors the option of using an ISBN or using their proprietary number. This option is free, and books printed with these will not be accepted for sale on Amazon or by any other store. (In fact, her objective is to prevent these books from being sold on Amazon.)

The fact is that virtually all books need an ISBN unless they fit with the above example.

Can you use the same ISBN for a book printed by both KDP Print and IngramSpark?

Yes, if the trim size and format are the same. In fact, this is the case regardless of who prints your book. (That is, if the dimensions are the same and both are paperbacks. Of course, you need a separate ISBN for a hardcover and KDP Print does not print hardcovers.)

3. Making changes to your book or unpublishing

Once an ISBN is assigned to a book, it is never reused. That's because all the information associated with the book, notably book reviews, reference that specific ISBN.

If you use a previously assigned ISBN for another book, that book will show those book reviews. There are hundreds of databases that store book information using the ISBN and those cannot be changed.

Fixing errors, changing contents, new editions

Changing your book cover: This does not require a new ISBN as long as the title remains the same.

Changing text or information inside the book: The official position within publishing is that fixing things like typos, grammar, and hyperlinks does not require the assignment of a new ISBN. As the pirate Barbosa said to Elizabeth in *Pirates of the Caribbean*: "The code is more what you'd call 'guidelines' than actual rules."

There are no formal consequences if you make lots of changes. There is no central authority that reviews the changes you make and enforces compliance.

It is more about you and your reader, meaning, you probably should make it clear to a book buyer that an edition is new and updated. Assigning a new ISBN is the clearest way to do this. Just keep in mind that any accumulated reviews may stay with the old edition.

However, have you noticed that some books with multiple editions—notably self-published nonfiction books on Amazon—have scores of reviews and many of those pre-date the most recent edition's release date?

For example, *Silent Sales Machine* by Jim Cockrum is in its 10th edition with 686 reviews (as of this writing). Not bad for a self-published book on the market for eighteen months.

However, if you sort the reviews by the date they were posted, you would see that 588 reviews were posted before the 10th edition's release date of August 11, 2017.

As shown in the next screen shot, the total number of reviews, regardless of what edition they apply to, are the same for all editions in this case. A shopper considering this book is no doubt impressed with hundreds of reviews and figures it must be the book to buy.

10th edition: August 2017

Here is a screen shot of Jim Cockrum's 10th edition in paperback format, released in August 2017. In this case he chose to use the free CreateSpace ISBN and the book shows 686 reviews even though only 98 are for this edition.

Product details

Paperback: 154 pages
Publisher: CreateSpace Independent Publishing Platform; 10 edition (August 11, 2017)
Language: English
ISBN-10: 1548401390
ISBN-13: 978-1548401399
Product Dimensions: 8.5 x 0.4 x 11 inches
Shipping Weight: 14.6 ounces (View shipping rates and policies)
Average Customer Review: ★★★★☆ ⌄ 686 customer reviews
Amazon Best Sellers Rank: #147,350 in Books (See Top 100 in Books)

9th edition: September 2015

Here is the 9th edition paperback edition of the same book, released two years prior in September 2015. It uses a different imprint name and ISBN, but the review count is the same as the 10th edition. (By the way, we can safely assume that this edition did not garner 588 reviews on its own. Rather, it inherited most of those from the 8th edition, and so on. A neat trick, indeed!)

Product details

Paperback: 102 pages
Publisher: JimCockrum.com; 9 edition (September 24, 2015)
Language: English
ISBN-10: 0692516603
ISBN-13: 978-0692516607
Product Dimensions: 8.5 x 0.2 x 11 inches
Shipping Weight: 12.6 ounces
Average Customer Review: ☆☆☆☆☆ ⌄ 686 customer reviews

Is this unethical or does it violate any laws or Amazon policies? It appears not. Let's consider who might be harmed.

- **Readers**: No harm in my mind, in fact they could benefit because it might be possible to download the most current eBook edition for free. And those buying the print edition know exactly what edition they are getting, assuming the ISBN was not reused for the next edition.
- **Retailers, resellers, wholesalers**: Only Amazon sells Kindle eBooks and they cannot be

resold. Since the print book got a new ISBN, other retailers are selling the most current book.

- **Author-publisher**: All those hard-earned reviews remain accumulated for their book and continue to grow in strength as social proof—a marketing engine for the new edition.

The most important point to make about attempting to do this is you should never reuse an ISBN for a print edition. It is indeed an easy matter to reupload a new file to KDP Print and/or IngramSpark to replace the previous content, but you should not do this.

Imagine you are a reader shopping for a used version of such a book. You would never know what edition you are buying! Since the ISBN is the same, it could be any one of several editions. There is a permanent market for used print books, and an ISBN is the only way to differentiate one edition from another.

True, it is possible for a shopper to buy an old edition—perhaps because of a low price and the mistaken impression that all those reviews are for that edition—but this seems unlikely to me. Most publishers clearly label the cover with an edition number after the first edition.

This is why the ISBN is so important. It helps readers and retailers differentiate between editions of a book. Never reuse an ISBN.

Unpublishing and reselling books

Another source of confusion and frustration for new publishers has to do with unpublishing a book. This is a simple matter for eBooks—you do indeed just unpublish the book. This is possible because eBooks cannot be resold.

Technically, eBooks are *licensed* to readers for their personal use. You are essentially paying a one-time licensing fee; you did not buy the book in the conventional sense of the word. So when you, the publisher, decide you no longer want to sell an eBook, you unpublish it. There is no aftermarket for eBooks.

Contrast this with print books. A book owner's right to resell or giveaway their copy is protected by law. It's called the law of first sale and it permits book owners to sell their copy. (United States law; your country's laws may differ.)

The ISBN helps facilitate this. As the book's owner, you can sign-up with Amazon's SellerCentral (or eBay, etc.), enter the ISBN with the price you want to sell it for, and sell the book. The publisher cannot stop you.

As far as print books are concerned, the ISBN is permanently assigned to that specific book.

4. Sharing an ISBN or multiple versions of the same book

An ISBN cannot be shared; you need an ISBN for each version, or edition, of a book—or if you change the format (replace your hardcover with a paperback). Here are a few examples that each require a unique ISBN:

- Hardcover
- Paperback
- Hardcover or paperback in a different language
- Color version of the hardcover
- eBook (if you decide to assign an ISBN)
- Stuffed toy character based on your book★

Note that the same book printed by different printers does not need a different ISBN. So yes, use the same ISBN for both KDP Print and IngramSpark assuming they share the same dimensions and are both paperback—and the ISBN is not the free one provided by KDP Print.

★Yes, that stuffed toy could get an ISBN! Many of us might recall the days before Amazon when there were bookstores in every community, selling all sorts of products related to or based on books such as games, stuffed animals, puzzles, etc.

In those days—before the world standardized on Universal Product Codes—stores needed a way to track all products sold in a bookstore, not just books. The ISBN was used for that purpose.

5. Costs and sources

In the United States, which this book focuses on, there is a fee. If you want your publishing imprint name to show as the publisher, you need to buy your ISBN from Bowker's MyIdentifiers.com website, or one of its authorized sellers such as Amazon KDP Print and IngramSpark.

ISBN pricing as of 2020

Direct from Bowker's MyIdentifiers.com website:

- 1 ISBN: $125
- 10: $295
- 100: $575
- 1000: $1,500

 TIP: Members of The Independent Book Publishers Association get a 15% discount.

Authorized resellers (and there are others besides these two):

- KDP Print: $99 for 1, no quantity discount
- IngramSpark: $85 for 1, no quantity discount

ISBNs are issued based on the location of the publisher. If you are in Canada, get your (free) ISBN from the authorized Canadian agency. See the section on selling internationally for links to these and other international agencies.

What if you need just one ISBN?

In my experience the primary reason to buy a single ISBN from an authorized reseller is simplicity. There is no need to stop what you are doing on Amazon or IngramSpark to set up an account with MyIdentifiers to buy a single ISBN. And neither Amazon KDP Print nor IngramSpark are set up in a way for you to shop for a single ISBN—buying one is part of the publishing process.

6. Branding and ownership

It would be cool if we could partner up with fellow authors to buy one hundred ISBNs and then share them, right? No so fast.

Whether you buy 1 or 1,000, those ISBNs are assigned to a single account holder. While it is possible to have more than one imprint assigned to a single MyIdentifiers account, it requires coordination if you plan to share.

Most publishers, including self-publishers, buy and manage their own ISBNs. As I mentioned earlier, you can mess up a book's online listings if you accidentally assign the same number to two different books.

The name of the publishing imprint is assigned to each number. If you keep this straight you won't have a problem and your branding will stay consistent.

When you log into MyIdentifiers, go to the imprint page and add a new imprint. When you assign an ISBN to a book, make sure it is the correct imprint.

Once you submit the book's information as final, that's it. If you make a mistake or want to change it, you'll need to assign a new ISBN.

7. SEO and discovery

I divide the search engine optimization (SEO) and discovery (a book's findability online) benefits into two categories:

1. **Amazon:** Your publishing imprint name is searchable on Amazon. If you chose a unique name, and market it (so that people are looking

for it), your books will show up when that imprint name is typed in the search box.

2. **Other:** When it comes to books, Amazon is the undisputed destination for most shoppers. As I mentioned earlier, Google is attempting to bring more value to owning an ISBN by steering people looking for an ISBN to the publisher, but this is an uphill battle.

Bottom line: I don't believe owning an ISBN currently brings any measurable SEO value outside Amazon. The exception might be for larger publishers or those with lots of books.

8. Selling internationally and foreign languages

You need just one ISBN to sell your book anywhere in the world. The only time you need a different ISBN is if:

- Your book is translated into a different language.
- Your book's publisher name changes.

A book available in the different online stores in Europe—whether this is via KDP Print, IngramSpark, or any other wholesaler or distributor—does not need a different ISBN.

But let's say you give permission to a publisher in France to sell the English edition of your book. They can assign their own ISBN or use your ISBN. In practice they would most likely assign their own ISBN to make it easier to keep track of sales.

It's worth noting that there might be some advantages to getting an ISBN issued by the agency in the country where you plan to sell. For example, a publisher based in another country will need a U.S.-issued ISBN from Bowker to get a Library of Congress Control Number (LCCN) in the U.S.

(I go into detail about registering with the Library of Congress in my reference book, *Register Your Book: The Essential Guide to ISBNs, Barcodes, Copyright, and LCCNs.* You can also visit the Library of Congress information page for more details: http://breve.link/mpi9

Selected sources for ISBNs outside the United States

Canada:
- English: http://breve.link/mpi10
- French: http://breve.link/mpi11

United Kingdom and Ireland:
- https://www.nielsenisbnstore.com/

Australia:
- http://breve.link/mpi12

Look up all other country agencies here:

- http://breve.link/mpi13

9. Distribution of ISBN information to other databases

According to Bowker, information about your book will be available to:

- 3,000 subscribers of the Books In Print and Global Books database.
- 1,800 library customers, including the New York Public Library, Harvard University Library, and the British Library.
- 5,000 libraries and branch locations.
- Retail customers including Barnes & Noble, Follett (college bookstores), and independent bookstores.
- School systems.
- Pubnet.org and PubEasy.com, e–commerce systems for the book industry.

I've mentioned that many small publishers see little value in the ISBN or don't see the value in following industry protocol for assigning the ISBN to a book. But is this a self-fulfilling prophecy?

How one indie publisher got wholesale orders and a book signing before the pub date

Here's a story I share in my reference book, *Register Your Book,* about the benefits of early ISBN registration.

This was a typical independent publishing scenario. It was our first book, and we were managing a myriad of details, including delays assembling metadata. Most notably, we lacked a PDF of the book itself, which prevented us from finalizing all the details until just a few weeks before its release.

I submitted all the relevant details to our MyIdentifiers account for each ISBN about seven weeks prior to the release date. Because most of our distribution was through online stores, I had a process in place to regularly search for the title and ISBN using Google and Bing.

Surprisingly, I came across a listing for the hardcover edition in the online store for the large South Florida bookstore group, Books and Books.

Up until this point the only public listing of the hardcover ISBN was through MyIdentifiers and Amazon. And since Amazon isn't in the business of notifying, much less supplying, competitors with information about new books, we can only assume the BooksandBooks.com listing came via Bowker's MyIdentifiers data feed.

The upshot was that we were able to contact the store and arrange a book event for the author. It didn't end there. Before the book was even released, we had orders from a wholesaler that serves libraries and schools. They contacted us because they found the book via the Bowker Books In Print database.

Clearly this might not happen for all books, but it does illustrate that there are markets for books beyond Amazon. If you do buy ISBNs, make sure all your book details are entered in the Bowker database accessible through MyIdentifiers.com.

7

KDP Print and IngramSpark

'____'ve already talked about the consequences of using a free ISBN for eBooks (#1 in the Chapter 6), so we'll focus now on print books which do require an ISBN in order to be sold in stores.

But before we talk specifically about KDP Print and IngramSpark, it is important to talk about other publishing options and how they relate to ISBNs. Here are a few situations you may come across:

- **Vanity publishers**. You will use their ISBN. Examples include Outskirts Press and Author-Solutions, and all the AuthorSolutions imprints: Xlibris, AuthorHouse, iUniverse, Trafford, West-Bow Press, Balboa Press, Archway Publishing, and Abbott Press.
- **Self-publishing services**. Publishing services companies allow you to use your ISBN or will

assign you one of theirs. Examples include Lulu, Blurb, and Bookbaby.

- **Book shepherds/publishing consultants**. Some individuals and small firms buy a series of ISBNs and then create an imprint nested under their imprint. See *Chapter 5, Golightly Publishing* for a screenshot of what this looks like in the Bowker account.

  If you go this route, keep in mind that the top-level imprint name may be the imprint that is displayed in some situations, rather than your imprint name.

- **Hybrid publishers**. In my experience, a legitimate hybrid publisher always uses the name of their imprint. You don't have a choice. This makes sense because one of the most valuable assets a hybrid publisher provides is book distribution and this relies on the reputation of the publisher—their imprint name. Notable examples include Greenleaf Book Group, Ink Shares, and She Writes Press.

The remainder of this chapter goes into detail about ISBNs when using KDP Print and IngramSpark.

KDP Print and ISBNs

One reason authors love KDP Print is that they offer a free ISBN. In fact, there is zero cost to publish a paperback book using KDP Print.

Format your book in Word, select the free KDP Print ISBN option, upload your files, and proof it online. If Amazon is the only company you ever plan to use for printing your book, you don't need to worry about ISBNs.

But what if your ambitions are larger?

- Maybe you'd like to market your book to libraries and you heard that getting an LCCN is helpful.
- Or what if you get an order for 1,000 copies and want to print them (far less expensively) by a different book printer?
- Perhaps your local bookstore agrees to host a book signing and wants to order them from Ingram, the industry-leading wholesaler for book retailers.
- Or maybe you decided, after publishing your book using a free KDP Print ISBN, that you'd like to publish more books and have those all in the name of your imprint.

Oops. You are out of luck if you used the free KDP Print or CreateSpace ISBN. You will need to re-publish your book with a different ISBN if you want to change the publisher name.

Here are a few reasons why this may matter:

Printing: The terms of your Amazon contract specifically state that KDP Print or CreateSpace must be your only printer. That means you cannot use the free Amazon ISBN at IngramSpark, nor may you use another printer to print your book.

Bookstore events: It's no secret that bookstores blame Amazon for syphoning off their customers. Telling them your publisher is KDP Print or CreateSpace is the kiss of death if you want a store to order books for a bookstore event.

Libraries: The Library of Congress assigns LCCNs to publishers, and since KDP Print or CreateSpace is on record as your publisher, you're out of luck.

Branding: You are doing more to build the brand of the KDP Print imprint ("Independently published") than your own publishing brand.

KDP Print gives you three options

KDP Print allows you to choose one of three ISBN options:

1. Use their free ISBN.
2. Purchase one for $99 (Amazon is an authorized reseller).

3. Use one you already have (purchased from Bowker or you got it from the agency for your country).

If you stopped reading now to visit KDP Print you'd likely get stumped at the consequences of choosing anything other than the free option. Amazon has an optional distribution program called Expanded Distribution and it changed when they transitioned from CreateSpace to KDP Print.

Expanded Distribution

Amazon made a signification *positive* change—at least in my opinion—when they transitioned from CreateSpace to KDP Print. It used to be that you had to use the free CreateSpace-assigned ISBN to get your book into the Baker & Taylor catalog, a former national book wholesaler to bookstores, libraries and academic institutions. This is no longer the case.

- You do not have to use the free KDP Print ISBN to qualify for Expanded Distribution. An ISBN you own or buy also works.
- Your book is listed in the Ingram catalog which is also used by libraries and academic institutions, in addition to bookstore retailers.

Your book must still meet certain trim-size requirements and you will get a lower royalty, but these have more to do with using another company, Ingram, who also needs to be paid for the services they provide. Learn more here: http://breve.link/mpi14

 IngramSpark offers trim sizes that Amazon's Expanded Distribution does not. If Expanded Distribution is important, it's probably better to not select this on Amazon and instead use IngramSpark.

Summary of KDP Print options

	Free KDP Print ISBN	Buy from KDP Print*	Bring your own
Cost	$0	$99	$1.50 to $125 each
Pros	• Free • Automatic entry into the Books In Print database • Fast! (little effort on your part/one less account)	• Low-cost if you want to buy just one • Branding control • Print anywhere • Register with Library of Congress • Simple to buy; no need to setup a new account with MyIdentifiers • Bookstores like you	• Cheapest if you plan to publish more books, or intend to assign an ISBN to an eBook • Ultimate control over your book's metadata • Branding control • Print anywhere • Register with Library of Congress • Bookstores like you

	Free KDP Print ISBN	Buy from KDP Print*	Bring your own
Cons	• Your published by name shows as "Independently published" • Can't print elsewhere • Can't register with Library of Congress • No branding • Brick-and-mortar stores won't order • Cannot be used at IngramSpark	• Another expense • Expensive if you plan to publish more books	• A larger upfront investment

★Amazon KDP Print is an authorized reseller of ISBNs.

KDP Print vs. CreateSpace publisher name

The new paperback option available from KDP is similar to CreateSpace but with one notable difference.

Instead of the publisher name showing as *CreateSpace Independent Publishing Platform*, a free ISBN from KDP Print will show the publisher as *Independently published*.

(This book only deals with ISBN and publisher name–related topics. There are other differences between CreateSpace and KDP Print, and you can read about them here: http://breve.link/mpi15)

IngramSpark and ISBNs

IngramSpark is KDP Print's primary competitor and in May 2020 they added a long-overdue ISBN option: free. What is more, IngramSpark has a special arrangement with MyIdentifiers that allows the publisher (you) to use an imprint name of your choosing (subject to my advice in Part 1).

The catch is the same as it is with the free KDP Print ISBN—it cannot be used with any other printer. You must print books using this free ISBN only at IngramSpark.

However, they too are an authorized reseller of ISBNs at $85 each. Of course, you can also supply your own.

One other point of differentiation is that you do not have to have an ISBN to print books. This is helpful if you do not plan to sell your book in retail stores; otherwise, an ISBN is required.

Instead, IngramSpark will assign their own internal stock tracking number. This free option enables you to buy books that you might give away or sell directly to the public at events or via your website.

Publishers also use this option when producing advance reading copies for soliciting early reviews and feedback. You can always buy an ISBN later if you change your mind.

As a reminder, buying an ISBN from IngramSpark is the same as buying it from MyIdentifiers.com. You, not IngramSpark, are the publisher of record. That means you could conceivably buy your ISBN from IngramSpark and use the same number at KDP Print, assuming the book's dimensions are the same and it's a paperback.

Authorized seller or bootleg?

How do you know if you are buying an ISBN that will name you as the publisher? I've seen websites selling ISBNs for $10 and $20 and claiming they are legitimate. You have two choices.

- Find out if you will have your own account at MyIdentifiers.com.
- Call MyIdentifiers and ask them: (877) 310-7333.

Don't be duped.

8

MyIdentifiers.com: Registering Your Imprint

If you bought your ISBN using CreateSpace, KDP Print, or IngramSpark, you can skip this section. Those companies have automatically registered your ISBN information with BooksInPrint.com (the database of print books maintained by Bowker).

Otherwise, you need to follow the instructions below. None of this is complicated or requires special knowledge, but it does require careful record keeping and attention to detail.

Account setup and buying the ISBN

This is easy except for one key decision.

1. Visit www.MyIdentifiers.com.
2. In the top right, click **Register**.

3. Assuming you are a new customer, select **I am a new Bowker Customer**.
4. On the **Create An Account** page, complete all the information except pause at…
5. **Company Name**: This is where you enter the publishing imprint you researched in Part 1. This is the name that shows as publisher once you assign an ISBN to a book.

I can't tell you how many people stumble on Step 5!

One of my clients learned this the hard way. Eager to get started, and before he had a plan, he bought his ISBNs. The problem is that he used his name, not knowing that this would be the name of his imprint. Fortunately, we were able to get this corrected because the book was still in production and the ISBN was not formally assigned.

Don't panic if the wrong name gets entered. *Before you assign your first ISBN,* simply email their support team and ask to have it changed (pad@bowker.com).

For many new publishers, buying 10 for $295 is the most economical, but it depends on your publishing plans. During the purchase process Bowker will also try to sell you other services.

For example, one of those might be barcodes. These are unnecessary if you are using KDP Print or

IngramSpark because both companies will print the barcode for free during the book printing process (see my other book, *RegisterYour Book,* for more detail about barcodes or download my free Barcode Basics guide by visiting http://breve.link/mpibarcodebasics).

9

No or Low Budget, or Just Plain Going Without

If you want to sell your printed book on Amazon—or in any other online or brick and mortar store—it must have an ISBN. But as noted earlier, many printers and services providers will provide one for free.

Here are four ways to save money:

1. **Print books**: use the free KDP Print ISBN, or produce your book using a service like Lulu or BookBaby. Both of the latter provide a free ISBN and the means to list your book in the Amazon store (and other stores).
2. **eBooks**: You won't need an ISBN if you "go direct"—that is, use a store's self-service portal.

These are available from Amazon (KDP), Barnes & Noble, Apple, and Kobo.

3. **Use an aggregator**—a company that puts your eBook into several stores at once. They do require an ISBN but will provide one free. Consider Draft2Digital, Smashwords, Lulu, and BookBaby.

4. **Sell from your website**. That is, sell direct to the public like after a speech or for a workshop. Use IngramSpark and opt to use their internally assigned ID number. The books you produce cannot be sold in stores, but then maybe that's the point.

10

Summary of Key Topics

Congratulations for investing your time to learn about one of the most confusing steps in publishing. You would be surprised how many people skip learning about imprints and ISBNs only to discover—after their book is published—the consequences of their choices.

Do you have to buy your own ISBN and set up an imprint to publish successfully? No, of course not. But I hope I've helped you think about some of the reasons why you should consider it, and what it takes to make it happen should you decide to take these steps.

Let's recap the key points to consider:

1. Cost: If you want to use your own ISBN, in the name of your own imprint, the least you can spend is $85. Buy one ISBN from IngramSpark

or buy ten for $295 from MyIdentifiers.com. (See Chapter 6.)

2. Do not buy ISBNs from unauthorized sources. If you aren't sure you're in contact with an authorized source, call MyIdentifiers/Bowker to verify at (877) 310-7333. (See Chapter 7.)

3. If your goal is to spend as little as possible, and you don't care about the consequences, get the free ISBN from KDP Print or IngramSpark. (See Chapter 7.)

4. Naming your imprint: Pick something meaningful to you or your writing subjects. Check if anyone is using it or a variation. (Use the resources in Chapter 3.)

5. Do you have to setup a company or legal entity to use a publishing imprint name? No. Do this only if you plan to accept money in the name of your imprint. (See Chapter 2.)

6. Can you change the name of your imprint after you publish your book? No. You will have to use a different ISBN if you want to use a different name. (See Chapter 6.)

7. What are the disadvantages of a free ISBN from Amazon (or anyone else, for that matter)?
   - It is subject to certain use limitations—read the fine print. For example, you cannot use another printer if you are using the free KDP Print or CreateSpace ISBN.

- The name of the publisher will be the name of the person or business who originally bought the ISBN.
- You cannot get a LCCN. (See Chapters 1 and 7.)

8. Do you have to own an ISBN to copyright your book? No. An ISBN has nothing to do with copyright. (See Chapter 5.)

Three Final Things

Would you mind leaving a few words about this book in a review on Amazon, Goodreads, or wherever you bought it? It doesn't have to be long or detailed—the main purpose is to share your opinion. This helps other readers decide if my book might be valuable to them.

Thanks, I really appreciate it.

Once again, each time I release a book or training resource I offer everyone on my mailing list advance notice about an exclusive launch offer. If you'd like to get notified, please visit **DavidWogahn.com/join** to sign-up or subscribe to one of the free resources at AuthorImprints.com.

And finally, don't forget to grab your **free** Barcode Basics guide. Save your money and don't buy barcodes until you read this: http://breve.link/mpibarcodebasics.

Also in the *Countdown to Book Launch*™ Series

- Reference essential metadata details for ISBNs, barcodes, LCCNs, copyright.
- Avoid legal headaches, missed deadlines, and expensive fees.
- Learn how to publish as a professional, not an amateur.
- Protect your book's hard-earned reader reviews.
- Ensure your freedom to use any book printer.
- Include your book in the directories used by major publishers.
- Keep your options open to use any book distributor.
- Prevent your advance reading copies from being re-sold online.

Learn more at www.DavidWogahn.com/ryb

Book Reviews: Step One on the Road to Book Sales

Learn more at www.DavidWogahn.com/brc

Also by David Wogahn

The Book Reviewer Yellow Pages, 9th Edition
Successful eBook Publishing
Marketing and Distributing eBooks
(LinkedIn Learning)

The
Book Reviewer Yellow Pages

A Directory of 200 Book Bloggers,
40 Blog Tour Organizers and 32 Book Review Businesses
Specializing in Indie-Published Books

9ᵀᴴ EDITION

DAVID WOGAHN

Learn more at
DavidWogahn.com/bryp

Notes

1. Ingram Publisher Services [IPS] is a sister organization of IngramSpark. IPS also handles distribution for another well-known author-publishing imprint, Hyde Street Press, the imprint for Barbara Freethy's books. http://breve.link/mpi6

2. If you'd like to dive into the weeds on this topic, check out Book Industry Study Group Policy Statement POL-1101: "Digital books of differing file formats should be assigned different identifiers…," but that "…it is not always necessary that each identifier be an ISBN."

About the Author

D avid Wogahn is a LinkedIn Learning author and the author of five books including *Register Your Book* and *The Book Reviewer Yellow Pages*.

The content of his books draws from his in-depth experience as president of the award-winning author-services company AuthorImprints.com. AuthorImprints.com has helped more than 125 authors professionally self-publish books using their own publishing imprint.

During David's 30 years in publishing and online media, he has worked for the *Los Angeles Times*, the Los Angeles Olympic Organizing Committee, and was co-founder of the first online publisher of sports team branded websites known today as the CBS College Sports Network.

He is a frequent speaker and trainer, including presentations for the Independent Book Publishers Association (IBPA), the Alliance of Independent Authors (ALLi), the Independent Writers of

Southern California, and the Santa Barbara Writers Conference.

Contact David by visiting DavidWogahn.com or AuthorImprints.com.